CREATURE COLLEAGUES

I0757367

+ 50 HIGH QUALITY DESIGNS

The Fox

Clever and shrewd, but with a tendency to manipulate or withhold information

The Elephant

Natural leader with a commanding presence and an unwavering determination, able to recall information with remarkable accuracy and precision.

The Lion

Authoritative and dominant, with a tendency to prioritize their own needs over those of their colleagues, but with an impressive track record of success and a talent for overcoming challenges.

The Tiger

Intelligent and savvy, with a talent for navigating difficult situations and thinking on their feet.

The Owl

Wise and knowledgeable, but can be overly critical or pedantic.

The Gorilla

Powerful and imposing, but can be quick to anger and intimidating towards others.

The Penguin

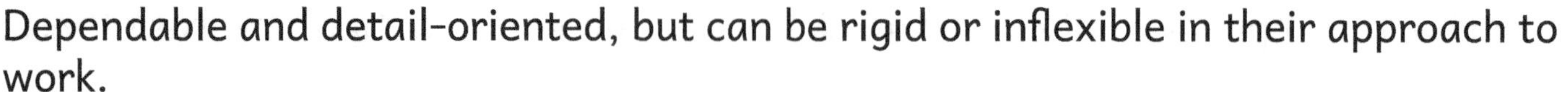

Dependable and detail-oriented, but can be rigid or inflexible in their approach to work.

The Octopus

Resourceful and adaptable, but can be difficult to read or understand, and may be prone to shifting loyalties.

The Koala

Calm and gentle, but may be slow to react or unassertive in group settings.

The Chimpanzee

Intelligent and social, but may be prone to drama or conflict within the team.

The Bald Eagle

Confident and powerful, but may be overly aggressive or territorial with others.

The Shark

Focused and determined, but may be ruthless or cutthroat in achieving their goals.

The Giraffe

Graceful and patient, but may struggle to communicate effectively with others.

The Platypus

Creative and unique, but may be seen as odd or unconventional by their colleagues.

The Kangaroo

Energetic and enthusiastic, but may struggle to maintain focus on long-term projects.

The Crocodile

Strong and resilient, but may be seen as unpredictable or aggressive by others.

The Peacock

Confident and flamboyant, but may be seen as arrogant or self-centered by others.

The Armadillo

Tenacious and hard-working, but may be overly cautious or resistant to change.

The Polar Bear

Strong and resilient, but may be seen as aloof or distant by their colleagues.

The Raccoon

Resourceful and adaptable, but may be seen as sneaky or untrustworthy by others.

The Cockroach

Resilient and adaptable, but may be seen as unappealing or unpleasant by some. They are highly resourceful and able to survive in a variety of conditions, but may be prone to causing disruptions or chaos within a group setting

The Duck

Easy-going and adaptable, but may struggle with assertiveness or making decisions.

The Hippopotamus

Powerful and formidable, but may be prone to stubbornness or a lack of flexibility.

The Jellyfish

Graceful and ethereal, but may be seen as indecisive or passive by their colleagues.

The Lemming

Trusting and cooperative, but may be seen as overly dependent or naive by their colleagues.

The Mantis

Focused and determined, but may be seen as aggressive or confrontational by others.

The Ostrich

Adaptable and resilient, but may struggle with risk-taking or innovation.

The Peacock Spider

Flashy and flamboyant, but may be seen as attention-seeking or superficial by others.

The Quokka

Friendly and sociable, but may struggle with prioritizing work over socializing with colleagues.

The Rhinoceros

Strong and powerful, but may be prone to impulsiveness or a lack of foresight.

The Scorpion

Tough and resilient, but may be seen as intimidating or unapproachable by others.

The Uakari

Curious and playful, but may struggle to focus or stay on task for extended periods of time.

The Vulture

Efficient and resourceful, but may be seen as opportunistic or unsympathetic by others.

The Walrus

Dependable and hardworking, but may struggle with adaptability or change.

The Xerus

Agile and quick-witted, but may be prone to restlessness or impatience in group settings.

The Zebra

Adaptable and cooperative, but may be prone to indecision or a lack of direction.

The Dingo

Independent, protective, and territorial, but may be aggressive or difficult to train.

The Emu

Stubborn, territorial, and defensive, but may be skittish or easily frightened.

The Grey Wolf

Loyal, social, and protective, but may be seen as aggressive or confrontational.

The Ibex

Agile, sure-footed, and adaptive, but may be solitary or cautious around others.

The Jaguarundi

Solitary, adaptable, and elusive, but may be hard to read or predict.

The Lemur

Agile, playful, and curious, but may be easily distracted or unpredictable.

The Donkey

Dependable, hardworking, and patient, but may be seen as stubborn or resistant to change.

The Peregrine Falcon

Fast, efficient, and predatory, but may be seen as intimidating or unapproachable.

The Dog

Loyal, friendly, and eager to please, but may be seen as overly dependent or lacking in confidence. They thrive on social interaction and may become anxious or unhappy when left alone for long periods of time. However, their loyalty and affection make them excellent companions and valued members of any team.

The Cat

Independent, curious, and adaptable, but may be seen as aloof or uninterested in socializing with others. They value their alone time and may become easily overwhelmed in a noisy or chaotic environment. However, when they form a bond with someone, they can be fiercely loyal and affectionate

The Manatee

Peaceful, gentle, and curious, but may be slow-moving or unassertive.

The Horse

Independent, loyal, and hardworking, but may be seen as stubborn or resistant to authority. They value their freedom and may become restless or unhappy in a rigid or confining environment.

The Snake

Strategic and calculated, but may be perceived as sneaky or untrustworthy. Can adapt to any situation and always seems to find a way to get what they want. May have a tendency to be overly competitive or secretive.

The Northern Saw-whet

Meticulous and detail-oriented, but may struggle with communicating effectively with others due to their shy and introverted nature. Has a great sense of intuition and is able to identify problems quickly, but may need help with taking action to resolve them. Can be fiercely loyal to their team and is always willing to help out when needed.

Snow Leopard

Independent and self-sufficient, but may struggle with working in a team or asking for help when needed. Has a keen sense of observation and is able to spot opportunities that others might miss, but may need help with executing their ideas. Has a calm and composed demeanor that can be reassuring in high-pressure situations, but may come across as aloof or unapproachable.

The Whale

Wise and experienced, but may have difficulty adapting to new or unfamiliar situations. Has a strong sense of empathy and is able to connect with others on a deep level, but may struggle with setting boundaries or saying no. Is a natural leader and is able to guide others towards a common goal, but may need help with delegating tasks or accepting feed-back.